#10048 $850

Part of the Deeper Sea

Other Books by *LOIS MARIE HARROD*

Every Twinge a Verdict
Crazy Alice

Part of the Deeper Sea

poems

LOIS MARIE HARROD

PALANQUIN PRESS
University of South Carolina–Aiken
Aiken, South Carolina

Copyright ©1997 by Lois Marie Harrod

Many of these poems first appeared in magazines: *American Poetry Review*:"Rabid Animals"; *Birmingham Poetry Review*: "Nunc Dimittis," "The Trumpeter Swan"; *Buffalo Bones*: "Grave Stele for a Little Girl, 450 B. C."; *Carolina Quarterly*: "The Tower of Babel," "Whites"; *Circumference*: "Bill Traylor's Dog"; *Coastal Forest Review*: "Figurative Speech"; *Confluence*: "Denying They Have Been," " Women of Uncertain Age"; *The Dickinson Review*: "Cormorant," "Equinox"; *Epiphany*: "That Same Prayer"; *Fine Madness*: "Birches," " Inside Nothing Is Resurrected"; *Journal of New Jersey Poets*: "Poster from a Photography Exhibition"; *Kalliope*: "Listening to God"; *The Literary Review*: "Horseshoe Crabs"; *The MacGuffin*: "Nor Ask How Many Wolves the Morning Ferns"; *More Than Animals*: "Blue Butterfly," "Holding the Dog"; *Passages North*: "Coming Backstage After a Young Man's Performance," "Henry Moore's *Three Motives Against a Wall*'; *Poet Lore*: "Doctor Sweetheart," "Three Windows"; *Poetry Digest*: "High Places"; *Prairie Schooner*: "M. C. Escher's *Day and Night,*" "Tongues"; *Second Glance*: "Green Snake Riding"; *The Snail's Pace*: "Mackinaw Wool Vest"; *Southern Poetry Review*: "Ice Storm"; *The Sow's Ear*: "Loitering in Air," "Teeth"; *Tamaqua*: "Corpus Canis," "Pieces of Montana Floating Past"; *Welter*: "White Bear"; *Zone 3*: "Bats in Mercury Vapor Lamplight."

The author wishes to thank Stephen Dunn, US 1 Poets Cooperative and especially her editor Phebe Davidson.

Published by PALANQUIN PRESS
    Department of English
    University of South Carolina–Aiken
    Aiken, South Carolina 29803
    All rights reserved.
    Printed in the United States of America.
    First printing, 1997.

Library of Congress Cataloguing-in-Publication Data
    Harrod, Lois Marie
    Part of the Deeper Sea: poems/ by Lois Marie Harrod.

ISBN 1-889806-18-8(cloth) ISBN 1-889806-15-3 (paper)
    1. Title
    2. Women's Studies

Library of Congress Number 97-065975

Table of Contents

Horseshoe Crabs	3
Burdock in Winter	5
Teeth	6
Tongues	8
Meditation on Redundancy	9
Equinox	11
Doctor Sweetheart	13
Denying They Have Been	15
Ice Storm	17
Bats in Mercury Vapor Lamplight	19
Corpus Canis	20
White Bear	22
Cicada	23
Coming Backstage After a Young Man's Performance	24
Pieces of Montana Floating Past	25
The Yellow Skunk Cabbage: *Lysichitum Americanum*	26
Blue Butterfly	27
Villanelle	28
The Bird Watcher	29
High Places	30
Figurative Speech	32
Nunc Dimittis	34
Dolphin Snow and My Father's Voice	36
Listening to God	37
Inside Nothing Is Resurrected	40
Holding the Dog	41
Grave Stele of a Little Girl, 450 B.C.	43
Dark Abstraction	45
Three Windows	47
Mackinaw Wool Vest	49
Nor Ask How Many Wolves the Morning Ferns	51
The Trumpeter Swan	52
Whites	53
The Tower of Babel	54
M. C. Escher's *Day and Night*	55
Pelvis	57
Cormorant	59
Birches	61

Poster from a Photography Exhibition	63
Bill Traylor's Dog	65
Henry Moore's *Three Motives Against a Wall*	67
Green Snake Riding the Back of the Kitchen Chair	68
Rabid Animals	69
The Sky Like Cobblestone	71
That Same Prayer	73
Turning Fifty	76
Women of Uncertain Age	78
Vending Machine	79
The Dynamics of Cold	80
Tod und Leben	82
Departure	83
Loitering in Air	86
A Note About the Author	88

Part of the Deeper Sea

for Lee

Horseshoe Crabs
Brigantine Wildlife Refuge

It was not my day for love or death,
        and so I felt aloof, distant,
watching the horseshoe crabs

churn the bottom of their sandy basin
        as if the shore were a halfway house
and not part of the deeper sea.

The gulls too were there, black-headed
        and cackling, but they moved away,
scared from their own observations

when we stopped, you and I, to watch.
        Are they mating, you asked,
tens and twelves of crumpled shells

grinding over each other as if
        they were World War I helmets
deprived of bodies and so

in some platonic fashion were seeking one other
        as cerebral as themselves.
Then we noticed their widely spaced eyes

riding their carapaces like small glass beads
        seeming to see what they were banging
from any angle, each spike rising

at the base of its cephalothorax like a toy cannon.
        They did not seem to be hurting themselves,
though as I watched them, bouncing off each other

like bumper cars at a carnival,
        making curious glubbing sounds
as if the brain's glue were dolloping out of a cranial case,

I thought of the way my cerebrum seems to sound,
        separated from my body and living on its own,
as it does after we have been making love or fighting

and all my affection crawls off to a dented pot
        in the kitchen drawer.
I remembered then that they are arthropods

twisted out of the same armor that we were twisted once
        and I remember that afternoon and that night
our son, and then our daughter, were conceived,

how even as my own small body made
        its smaller, unpredictable shudder,
that this time, death had some purpose

and perhaps the steel tanks shearing across the sand
        had some purpose too, though nothing
I could claim. So we walked on, the gulls descending

to tear at the crabs that had bellied-up on the shore,
        the ones that could not return to the water
except as some sporadic heckling.

Burdock in Winter

Perhaps no one could have saved
the yellow-crowned kinglet
fixed like a thief. Nevertheless,
these are my excuses:

I was a season late,
I did not know his name,
I could name the thistle.
You see one does not

walk out to find that a wing
as light as light cannot extricate
itself. I wanted what
I always want, salvation.

I wanted the burdock before the fall,
the salutary catch, the seed.
I would have freed him
so that I did not find him now,

dead and dry and nameless,
I did not want to know
that once pinioned,
he was too torn to fly.

Teeth

Summer, the dentist had sent
his final reminder, and her husband
wanted to make love in the morning
before she brushed her teeth.

What was there to stop her?
Their son was collaring opossums
in Carolina and their daughter
studying humpbacks on the Jersey shore.

But she had read about some rare disease
in which plaque grows so quickly
that the molars fall out in chunks.
Please, she said, her mouth becoming the bowl
in which her daughter's fish had died.

No, she didn't want more fish
but he remembered, didn't he,
how she tried to find those magic crystals
to fill the bowl, the kind her mother
had bought her in Woolworth's once
when her own carp Goldie caught fin rot.

Now she wanted to fill the bowl with water,
pour in the box of colored pebbles
and the magic growing solution, and wait.
Twenty-four hours later, *voila*,
there would be an array of pink and green incisors
studding the the bowl like the teeth of a coelacanth.

Of course, Woolworth's didn't have those kits anymore
or those sea monkeys which would have come to life
if her mother had only let her purchase them,
and whatever her own daughter begged,
there was going to be no new puppy in this house
chewing up the brushes and no sore gums.

Please, she wanted to get up and wash
and hang out the sweaty pillowcases
and all the white towels in a row,
she wanted to mark them
like teeth on a dentist's card,
an X for every cavity.

Tongues

Sometimes when I am running
a car comes from nowhere
like a chariot and then
the trembling—

your bread in my mouth
words like new tongues
where does the body stop
the flesh begin?

Those banquets I remember
spoons full of peacock tongue—
I heard them squawking
from their red-tiled roofs

and yet I ate, their tails
splashing down like water
and all I saw
I gave to your mouth—

three tongues
riding the white iris throat
and you could taste
that little thorn of flesh

caught between the teeth.
It is the sun we must consider:
how to burn in November
how to breathe and breathe.

Meditation on Redundancy

Each breath
is a breath
within another breath,
he wrote
thinking of his body
held within hers
as she lay
within his arms.

And beyond his mouth
the double curtains
and the lake,
the wind scrawling
what must be written
a hundred times,
slanted one way
and then another.

He remembered
the embossed letters
she had sent,
the ones she turned
at right angles
and crosshatched
when she ran
out of space,
so hard to read.

But now
he could imagine
the first time

he had felt her
breath in the dark,
all air diminished
to a single scribble
against his cheek.

And the second.
And the second.

Equinox

At those deliberate moments when
dark becomes the twin of day
and midnight the altitude
of noon,

I hold two cups—
one your love,
smooth, glassy
as india ink;

the other light,
my own breathing.
On the kitchen scale
they weigh the same.

But when I pour them
into that white bowl
in which we make our bread,
who gauges loafing?

You never called me beautiful
though once you could have;
when you shudder it is Christ
not Eve you name.

I have spilled half my life
into a blackened vessel,
is it word or wind
you drink?

Sometimes I hold my tongue
as you cup water, I cannot remember
how much I have poured into your hand,
how much retained.

Doctor Sweetheart

Sometimes, beneath you, I want
to disassemble everything,
like the man who spends each day

taking apart his Studebaker
and putting it back it together,
the one happy schizophrenic

in psychiatric lore; I want
to slide under your body
as his doctors say he slides,

as if you were an automoton
I knew how to fix; I want the voices
that sing to him to sing to me,

the white voices of delicate flounder,
yeast swelling inside a waxy bag,
the soft voices of women, meet us

at the doughnut store—and I would go,
as this rare and curious mechanic goes
every afternoon to the corner bakery

where, because I do want to be happy,
I would refuse to remember
the asphalt pillow and labored wrench

that began me there, where I would not
be disappointed when you,
like his gentle voices, were not there to meet me,

where I would know, as he always knows,
that you had been there, that you had
just come and slipped away,
that I had only just missed you.

Denying They Have Been

When death comes
like a sudden snow
separating the sparrows
from their hungry song

and there is nothing left
to devour our silence
except the shovel grinding
the concrete porch,

love descends
like a white collar
and we hold our cries
in our throats like bees.

Outside the sleet
is stinging the lamplight,
inside the window glass
swells with sweat.

We have nothing left to say
but we spell so admirably
that after only a day or two,
a white hive drones.

When we walk
the field tomorrow
we will notice the weeds
with their bony fingers,

and think of foxes
keeping tally in the snow:
their red backs
and sudden paws

like lances
in some quick game
we did not ask
to know.

Ice Storm

The clouds are riding
a sky more like stretched canvas
than any blue

I've seen lately
in Magritte's Department Store,
and though they may be cursing

you for leaving me,
I have manufactured things
I could not dream in your presence:

blue machetes and paper fire,
loss in a dense forest
deep in El Salvador

where ill-painted leaves
resemble torrid shingles
or your hands.

We never saved each other,
though once, I remember,
we talked Antarctica in a warm, dim place,

and I rested my fingers on yours
briefly, lightly, as the cool shadow
that held your face.

I do not ask what you remember,
but this glacial morning,
the hemlock's wild thumbs

are gloved in ice.
So there it is,
the presumptuous metaphor

too hot to hold in this hemisphere
even if you can hear
such creaking, such cold desire.

Bats in Mercury Vapor Lamplight

The bats have set me softly down
in the suburban darkness

if I stay away much longer
you would worry as you do

when I strip the bed
down to its stained mattress

and forget the sheets
but I am afraid

the moths are becoming
syllables in my mouth

I am waiting
to see the bat again

the black orchid
over the Russian snow

all the things I do for you
when I do not know how to continue.

Corpus Canis

And when your dog returns
(not the pomeranian you hated
those seventeen years

and buried in the laurels,
a little white cross
stuck clean through

his pop-eyed heart,
but another, more dangerous
than any you control),

you wonder, the moon
full of clotted vinegar,
the sky black as a sock,

how you can enter these streets
where there are no lights
and only this dog to lead you.

You think of the man
who leaped before your car
that night in the rain storm,

his slick hairless chest,
how he spat at you
when you swerved and missed.

You think it must be his shirt
hanging from a wet tense wire
that brings the floodlights down

and yet you are out in the darkness
with this uncertain breed, the dog
you refuse to love,

the dog whose teeth could take
your neck, and you do not understand
why he wants to be led by you.

White Bear

Some morning before the black alarm
I want you to wake speechless

and take the dog whose mouth
is tied with black ribbon

and go with me into the cool
December silence where all is spent

but the morning star hanging
like a bronze balloon in an oriental dream.

We will wear the leather shoes
that do not echo beyond the horizon

and the dog will trot obedient
as if she were a white bear

and all her duty to guide us
to that east that now begins.

Cicada

Sometimes on fences
you come upon their deeper skins,

a man waking from desire,
a woman folding gauzy wings,

you read the tissue you could have written,
the husk and its unspoken vowel,

ravens sifting through the windows,
words splitting shadows on a wall,

the green sun falls as grass in fields,
the roots reveal themselves,

two chestnuts and a dappled oak
but someone has stolen the book of trees.

You cannot name the boy's wet shoulders,
you cannot name the girl's bright skin,

but you come upon them
as you come upon yourself

climbing a hill, your heart a parchment,
the last mist breathing below.

It is not noon. It is not midnight.
It is morning dropping its papery shell.

Coming Backstage After a Young Man's Performance

His shoulders quivering as if rain
running off his collar bone, his mouth
mumbling something from the play,
how was it, madam, how liked you this?

And how do I answer, his skin flashing
like sheet lightning, body naked to his jeans.
He is no actor yet, but he has racked the dark
and distant barn, the willow bends like a girl in heat.

Perhaps years ago when I was seventeen and my flesh
the wet electric, there was someone too old for me
drowning in the wings—one who would not touch
and did not say, you, my child, your body . . .

I want that crooked old gaffer now, I want to hear
what I was too young to hear, how for a brief moment
my flesh too held bright as any word, art
be damned: I want him desperate while I breathe.

Pieces of Montana Floating Past

That fair night in another room
the moon dangled her black balloon
behind white trees

and the white dog sprang circles
so that I could not catch
her ebony teeth

pricking pinholes in Orion's belt.
I slung the onyx around
my waist, buckled,

and the air was suddenly thick
with the wet black odor
of brambles.

The Yellow Skunk Cabbage: *Lysichitum Americanum*

Below the ravenous migration of birds the skunkcabbage rises
like love breaching its yellow spathe. You can not mistake

its thick stalk and its thousand gold coins. It is
the bald eagle nesting his Midas, the steelhead

scrooging her hoard upstream. Of course, it recalls
certain prophetic rods and the sour scent of t-shirts,

Jane's adolescent addiction and Jim's crude fly silk-screened:
it is why we are here, the stinging pocket of burn and decay,

but we must not in early spring confuse it with the false
    hellebore
whose pleated leaves are stalkless and poisonous on their
    elongated stem.

Come summer the black bear devours it, roots and leaves,
and we can too, all of it, if we are careful, if we roast and dry,

if we purge its young leaves in bitter boils of potted water:
there is nothing here that we cannot contain.

Blue Butterfly

I have been thinking about the panic the larva must feel
as she stops feeding for no apparent reason
and begins to wander aimlessly unaware

of what she is seeking and what she is secreting—
that honeyed fluid that predicts the dark world of ants
who will come to her edges and carry her off,

a curled carcass, to their catacombs;
I have been thinking of the sadness she must know just before
she vanishes completely from her breeding place.

I have always understood her frantic certainty that she will die
just as she becomes the honored guest, just as the ants
begin to feed their grubs on the sweet ooze of her skin

and all that is left of her body begins to constrict,
but now I have been wondering what, if anything,
she will comprehend if, in the spring,

that inexplicable hysteria smears over her again:
will she just hunker down in her black chrysalis
or will she split out into air where suddenly
she will spin upwards on dry blue wings?

Villanelle

The moss has flung itself, a pale green scarf,
across the nest of speckled sparrow
since you lay beside me, drowning in the dark.

The moon's diminished in my mouth; its boulevard
of discs, an empty paten, and far below
the sea has flung itself, again, a pale green scarf,

across the sand and unravelled, and the green barge
you bore me on has sunk its flimsy snow
since you lay beside me, teasing in the dark:

"What is between us and what beyond the leopard
and his sister Death, I do not know."
The moss has flung itself, a pale green scarf

across the bed where the wild goose guards
the long-necked goslings (my mouth is full of slow
pillowing since you lay beside me, downing in the dark),

and I do not think you will ever say how hard
it has been to grow green, how hard to grow stone:
the moss has flung itself, a pale green scarf
since you lay beside me, leaving in the dark.

The Bird Watcher

The water is still there, leaking into her shoes
as she walks the field where once, at dusk,
her body begging death, she stopped, undressed—
how often had he asked her what she lacked?

And the darkness too, the smell of sphagnum
beneath her binoculars, water trickling through the roots,
and in a tree, a crow more like a rag than an omen:
she had lain down on her back to wait.

Now he strokes her hair as if it were a limp bird,
the black swan she had shot once accidentally
thinking it was a common goose—
she wonders what will happen if he leaves.

Something a boy might do, he had comforted,
mistake a woman for a common slut,
but she had seen what she had done,
the feathers black and clotted in the sun.

She had sworn off shooting then,
carried the heavy body from the swollen weeds
into the kitchen where she sat
three hours, stroking it in the dark.

High Places

She had studied aerial photographs of high places,
inaccessible plateaus rising thousands of feet
from the desert floor, had read
they were inhabited by weasel, mouse and shrew,
but no one knew how they got there,
so she set out to discover for herself.

There were difficulties, of course,
paths that seemed to ascend
levelled out and returned to the plain,
trails narrowed into deer tracks
and disappeared.

She dozed on the mossy side of trees,
dreaming that she had been in the wilderness
forty years though she had been gone
only two days, and her backpack
seemed to fill with stone tablets.

Somewhere above the tree line
the world changed, there were few mice
and no weasels, but strangers who had no difficulty
making the climb appeared
and pointed out the five states
she should be observing from the peak.

And then she didn't stay as long as she wanted:
just as she thought she might begin to understand
how falcons could light on the hardest rock,
and goats almost live on stone, she looked

on all that lay below and was hungry,
and it was time to think of coming down.

Figurative Speech

When we talked metaphor in my family,
we talked feet, how my mother's were clodhoppers,
and my father's so small, a lady's foot—

comparisons that made me wonder as I scuffed
into the kitchen in my father's shoes
why he said they were down in the *hill*.

We were poor, but our house was top of the road,
and he went down to Baltimore to buy the repair kit
that made the cellar smell of hard rubber and acetone.

I watched him hammer the cleats into the heels
so that they made dents in the linoleum,
which my mother said were like sin and could never be
    removed.

Nevertheless, he liked to be with us
on Saturday evenings when he finished his sermons,
and so he shined his shoes, carefully, on the table

while my mother curled our hair and polished our nails
according to the latest style, which meant slicking bright red
onto the tips but leaving the little moons naked and pale.

That's why I asked my Sunday School teacher Mrs. Sweeney
if she thought the moon in my thumb would rise
like the moon in the sky, and she said no, that was pure
    frippery

and wicked besides, and that's why that night I asked my
    father
if he thought the moon in the heavens was part of God's
    little finger,
and he said no, no, as if he were offended,

just as he had the evening he held my hand
and we saw the sun send shafts through the clouds,
the evening I said Daddy, it's Jacob's ladder,

the evening I told him the angels were climbing
without getting splinters in their socks and he said no, no, no,
    no—
it is just the sun dropping beneath the *heel.*

Nunc Dimittis

My sister wept when the baby birds
she had been feeding, stuffing their
nameless craws with dog food,
died, one by one.

But I to whom sad feelings
seemed a strange species did not cry then
or later when my own cat Ebenezer
limped home

though I knew I should feel inconsolable,
and not even Grandpa Gottlieb's cancer
and the long car rides to Baltic made me weep
an honest tear, though by his end

I learned the fine art of dissembling
in the house of mourners and even
a sort of justice in mocking funeral guests
with short faces and redder wine.

Of course, what had really been moving me
those endless Saturday journeys
to Grandpa's death was the imaginary collision
through which I would live,

but everyone else including my sister would die,
though to be fair to myself, I did not
hear the metal shredding or the gasoline
prying open agony.

It would just happen: then I would be alone
walking from room to room, sitting behind
my father's desk, reading Masefield,
as he did, with deep feeling.

Dolphin Snow and My Father's Voice

And once, in a gray ocean of snow
        I asked the light
about her white dolphins. There were

so many of them, singing their steady song.
        Inside my window
the dog was shaking her collar

as if she were chasing a white shark.
        I sat remembering
a day when I was two,

my first winter, going to find fish
        in the garden
and drowning in a drift of snow.

All the heavy clothing my parents
        thought necessary
I am now discarding:

the heavy pants between my thighs.
        I have spent closets
stripping down to cold sweat.

I watch them now, taking care
        of each other, my father
having polyps cut from his vocal cords,

my mother, from whom
        I got my brains,
sorting the cutlery.

Listening to God
(after Stephen Dunn)

At first the irritation
of hearing my last name
pronounced incorrectly,
one hand still damp
from dirty dishes,
the other holding
the receiver in a sour
towel, baby
funking up
the hollow of my thigh,
and then the voice
from one more past,
insistent,
like a used car salesman,
do you know who I am,
breathing,
the first two syllables
of my name
floating again
like a white dove
on a baptised horizon,
and I remember,
the baby's small
fingers tearing
at the corner of my mouth
with ragged nails,
that night
wrestling in the dormitory
furnace room
when the custodian

stormed us,
his voice sad
and lonely like a lamp,
not Jake,
not Stephen,
the baby groveling
down my jeans,
not Matt, not John,
no, no,
of course, not John,
the small voice
still closing,
for Pete's sake,
Nancy,
the uniform
neatly folded
in the obituary column
of the Youngstown Vindicator,
blown up in Nam,
my knees buckling,
Nancy,
the second lieutenant
unable to speak
his name after all
these years, bastard,
so why can't you
just say it,
God, God, God,
his narrow back
mocking desire,
my God, my God,
remember, he said,
his voice going wet

like a forsaken bandage,
the night the music
turned slow
and I held you,
three fingers
pressed into
your spine,
and afterwards
the wet field
beyond the veranda,
and I can remember
whispering no,
how I knew then,
no, no,
I didn't want him,
how he did not ask,
how I could have
shattered him,
perhaps,
instead of
lying there
smeared
in his panic,
no, no,
I cannot
remember.

Inside Nothing Is Resurrected

And I do not know what to say about my brother
accumulating in the corners of the closet
except that to sweep him out would raise a dust.
You see how it is, a faded shirt corpsing behind the door

and when I arrive, the swish of lithium.
Yesterday at the supermarket, he heard a voice,
shrill like my old starched pinafore: "Why," he asked,
"were you always trying to act so grown-up?"

Cheese is cheaper than whole macadamias,
but everything floats at the meat-counter
where fluorescent lights incarnadine his wrist:
I don't suppose a little salt will save him either.

Holding the Dog

When her jaw that could destroy me
      quivers, I am glad, most days,
that I hold the leash and do not need

to watch any animal, my own or someone else's,
      die a dog's death, not even
the preposterous squirrel

who drags her boa through the wet grass
      until she reminds me of at least one
of your old girlfriends, the one that was

in your wallet, but sometimes, my shoulder
      jerked almost out of its socket
and a perfectly-manicured rodent

preening in a bush-tailed yard,
      acorn equidistant from the twin oaks
and from the dog I am holding,

something I do not want to know
      wants me to let go the leash,
to see what beast inhabits our house

and sleeps at the bottom of our bed,
      what she would do,
left to her instincts. I know

some, maybe even you, will say just one more
      of her bitch poems, but being left
as I have been left all my life, holding the dog,

I have found it is not at all like being left
        holding the bag or holding the baby.
As you know, I've never been able

to hold the line between us, and this isn't a hold-up
        or even a hang-up anymore,
just that I have never had enough horses or a candle.

Grave Stele of a Little Girl, 450 B.C.
(in memory of my student Kim McCrae)

Now I am thinking of you
as a child
holding two doves,
one in your hand
as if it is ready to fly off
and the other
gently to your body,
your left arm bent
and its split tail resting
on your belly
which seems
slack and childish,
not the way it will become
as your body learns
the hardness of those horses
you so loved,
their flank and their speed.
You seem to be talking
into the mouth of your darling,
kissing it
as I imagine you did
those velvet nostrils
when you inserted the bit,
but there is something sad
in your eye
like a splinter,
as if you already know
the lid was painted once.
You have no belt
and your peplos is split

along the right side,
your arm, your buttocks
are rounded,
reminding me
how you were always
losing things,
belt, shirt, shoe, paper,
how birds fluttered
to and from your hands.

Dark Abstraction

The afternoon closes like a swollen eye
and I think of other ways to enter earth:

through the white pelvis on a winter day,
the sky dropping its blue egg,

or later at the horizon, a broken shell.
You are worried about your father

in a hospital a continent away,
wondering if you should go tomorrow.

Leave now, I say, remembering
the night you thought my grandmother too far

and the day I took chocolates
to the nursing home, my father saying,

"She won't get any, the nurses eat it all."
Everything is emptied by our gestures,

the sun dribbling darkness into that crevice
which light can never fill.

I remember my grandmother
in her last harsh fluorescence,

a bandaged bird who could no longer pour
her body through the canyon.

I see white hands pulling
at your father's boots.

Leave now, I say, and you sigh,
closing down your fingers with your eyes.

Three Windows

Let us begin with morning, light
coming through three windows,
the first a pane of glass and in
its mouth the moon, a platter too
big for its meager breakfast.

Smile, says the boy, that I
may have a face like yours, that I
may run my tongue along the gables
and smell wood smoke from each
house as if I had the nostrils
of a god.

      And the second pane, the air,
such flex of naked willow tangling
flights of string, any number
of twigs crossing clouds so pink
and sentimental that the sky
catching their reflection in
shallow pools can not trust one
of them.

      And the third window, the crack
of cold, the slit of the sheet where lovers
leave the bottom of the night, the window
with sharp edges where someone
is breathing across the neck of a flask.

Perhaps he needs a woman, perhaps
a man blowing around his neck
a scarf as hollow as wind, his eyes

behind his glasses, sharp as piccolos,
can he make sense of flesh, can he
imagine the body resolving like the moon
pressing its face so flat against
each window that the sky opens
empty as an empty bowl.

Mackinaw Wool Vest

He is the lumpish man at the bottom of the page
modeling one of those Mackinaw wool vests
that come in heavy black checks or solid gray
and he has his legs spread as if he were
Clay County Minnesota's answer to Paul Bunyan
and so I ask him where is he standing, is it
the meadow I know in Yellowstone or is it
his back lot in Fryeburg, Maine, where his brother
has dropped a light meter and squints into the sun.

And then, of course, I begin to undress him
because he looks hot and heavy and embarrassed
and I ask him what's under the Mackinaw wool vest,
is it the port wine birthmark he promised,
and he says that the shirt is the lightest green cotton,
only 26 dollars and that the temperature is 88 degrees,
he's sweating so profusely now that I will not be able
to scrape the fabric from his skin.

And so I tell him, you are like the rest, the ones
I almost remember from my Sears and Roebuck days
when the men I chose were catalogued and glossy,
and I counted myself lucky to find one barrel-studded chest
whose paper torso could hide under the shirts I clipped.

I tell him to hold out his paper hands, I think
they match ones I saw in a blue gabardine suit
before we met, I ask him whether I could just
scissor off his elbows so he can wear anything
or whether he would like to dance with me,

each of his six arms oddly angled as an Indian god
and each in a differently shaded sleeve.

Nor Ask How Many Wolves the Morning Ferns

It was enough that year
to lie without listening
to the moths falling against the moon

It was enough
to give no explanations
to the sun howling in the wood

A jackdaw's beak
clacked some old tale
about the upper limb of a bow

and I climbed the shaft
that was sent singing
into the bear that swallows dawn

The Trumpeter Swan

. . . and she twists her white swan neck, not as I would do
to see myself in the water, but to rest it down her back
as my neck might rest if it were turned by someone,

I do not think it would be you, someone who did not
know the limits of sand or water and so could draw my neck
into a narrow glass or a tulip stem and lay it so gently

down my spine that the woman who turned to salt, seeing it,
would remember her own throat that narrow evening
the blue gazelle first came at dusk to lick her collarbone;

someone who could lay it so gently that, looking back at the
    place
from which you brought me and from which I can no farther
    go,
I too would find a mouth, black and smooth as a beak,

and black eyes that could see what lies behind me is not the
    past
but my own body, one wing held open like a ruffled peony,
feathers translucent as white bells in the sun's Gomorrah.

Whites

These are the whites I see today: a white line,
a white net, a tennis court, a Shinto priest sitting
in the center, his little white finger extended,
his eyes white crystal—someone has carved
a white inscription inside his bald head
which is whiter than my tongue.

I do not know why he is here,
perhaps this is a liberal arts college,
where white Volkswagens appear
on auditorium stages, and white panties
hover the heads of eminent lecturers
at prayer.

Perhaps it is religion I'm talking, the way
fat-faced priests drop white cassocks like pears,
the way I hear them falling like soft marble
from white pedestals, the way statuary washes gray
as the water in a glass used to swirl a brush,
a whole ocean twisted opaque
in the stir of a hair.

On the beach where a white moon breaks like a shell,
a woman with white hair says when you paint
you must paint white eggs, one fresh and one boiled,
and know the difference.

She says she will show me
the twenty-seven names of god.

The Tower of Babel

Maybe it was a joke: the whore from Shinar
who'd raised the whole brick crew
up the rope with her one word John.

Or Abraham or Abel or just plain Abe
begging the unbelieving woman in his tent,
please, Sarah, please, can't you just shut up.

Or my father who never told me
how his father died or maybe my mother
who kept the clipping in her purse.

Perhaps I was too young to know how God loved silence:
how a few construction workers shouting clay
could wreck an upper room and bring the tower down.

I began to hear the deaf man singing
and the dumb woman swaying on her porch:
look, in the shadow of the babble,
a green bird tangled in the tall green reeds.

M. C. Escher's *Day and Night*

At first it seems the white geese become
white by flying east into the night
and the black geese black by flying west,
and that the two towns set east and west
are mirrors of each other and that a man
walking east at dusk towards the town
of night might gradually fade until
he became a light in one of the windows.

Or at dawn this man having walked
all night might enter the black
cathedral and rest in the last pew
by the baptismal font where the sun,
if it rose, would rise through the rose window
and touch the back of his collar, lightly, or
at noon this man or his brother might trudge
west towards the town of day, his face
growing darker with each step. But

look: the sister elms do not match
precisely and the little cottage beside
night's canal has one less burr oak,
though four people stride day's bridge,
three walk the bright windmill,
two approach the poplars, not one
slides behind night's fence. And so

this man, if he stops in the middle of the page
going east or west and looks up, he
will see some of the white geese lunging
through the dark, their eyes white without

pupils, and he will see a light goose
darkening above him with neither eye nor feather
and he may not know whether this bird
is becoming field, or furrow becoming
feather, and he may ask what he
is becoming now that there is
neither moon nor day. And then it seems

white must become white geese
flying east and black black geese
flying west, and that the two men
set east and west against each other
are brothers and that the man walking
east towards the town of night will
gradually grow so light he becomes
the shade in his brother's window.

Pelvis
    (after Georgia O'Keefe)

Maybe to name you
would destroy my mouth—
as I have heard gods
violated by a vowel,

but do not say
when I paint
that I am just adding white
to open the vocal cords.

What I see through
the pelvic throat
is my body becoming
the cottonwood tree.

Look how it grows,
a chanterelle,
the armature
of a silent angel—

in any desert
you are the sage
that cannot
speak to me,

not so, not that
I can say it.
See where all
this innocence has led,

even women

who became satin doors
put up with men
chasing callas,

my tongue is the cactus
and the femur
its peculiar flute,
so why should I think of you

standing at the window
of a room
I enter now
as a logical dominion.

Surely I am not
the first to hold your name
in my mind
like a quill,

yet I wonder
if you know me,
coming up behind you as I do,
slipping my fingers

between your ribs,
touching the hem
of your hip—
the clouds are fading

like garments,
some so delicately
I might have shaded them
myself.

Cormorant

I believe in the intellectual life the way
I might in a tea shop in Calcutta, sitting
beside Kumar the hotel steward as he pens
a poem each morning, his plume of cigarettes
lying in a red wrapper beside his reluctant
tea—or the way I might, along the Mississippi
Delta, going there without you and suddenly
seeing a cormorant hanging out her black
neck like a stylus in the sun.

By noon her feathers would be dry and Kumar
would ask what I thought of his sonnet, the one
in English, and I would tell him that I have names
for what I've seen—water turkey, crow
duck, shark with teeth like ink—but not one
is right, there's nothing to her but her bones.

Yet she submerges herself, forty seconds . . .
fifty . . . sixty . . . and then the spiny shattering,
the catfish clawing smooth and sliding down
her craw as if she could apologize
for the piano not being tuned. Why
it was only yesterday you said your father
was a bookmaker, the way you might have said it
in a backriver bathhouse where
they confiscated my widow's weeds and wrapped
me in a sheet.

                But you still love me, and Kumar
replies that, of course, his dark friend Dakoo
is not famous either, but from time to time

he sells cartoons to a Bengali paper, and I
must come to meet him at the coffeehouse
where the bookstalls spill onto the pavement,
paperbacks in every conceivable language,
even the most reticent. I remember
near Baton Rouge a plane hit a cormorant
more or less accidentally. Kumar,
I say, it was the bird that lived, the plane that fell.

Birches

Slender
as young men
but whiter,
women
should not turn
to trees,
but maybe these
with their black scars
are women
who have
lost their limbs
or wanted
to grow tall
to take the moon.
What can we make
from our bodies,
a canoe to carry us
from room
to room?

Birches,
I do not want you
to remind me
of young men
or young women.

I want myself
walking among you,
neither breast nor bone,
but a hand holding
a light meter

in the vestibule
of sleeves.
The sun shingles
the nave,
I cut my hair
to float like a cross,
how blue the leaves.

What can hurt me now
stripped of tissue—
oh, birches,
your white thighs
and black tourniquets.

Poster from a Photography Exhibition

When she saw him again after all those years,
he seemed a poster for an exhibition she had missed,

perhaps the Göttingen Museum May 22nd through June 26th,
one photograph from all that hung those plastered rooms,

a torso so white and smooth she wondered
how the rest of his body had been displayed:

his feet perhaps wrapped around the rungs of a white kitchen
    chair
or turned up beneath his buttocks, his toes like ten soft keys.

She focused on what remained: a navel
unlike any dent her thumb could press,

a swelling as if someone had thrown a clot of bread
on his flat abdomen, and he had lain there

as it rose and had stamped the center
with the head of a small steel pin;

and then his flaccid sex which the camera had loved
more than the face she could never see,

a face which must have had dark eyes
like this man before her, perhaps hair already thinning—

and then she could see that this man before her
must have been a boy in some chalk-laden schoolroom,

his pen clamped between his lips as if the answer to the essay
were already in his mouth, his hair black and curly,

his tongue one she would have touched
if she had only known his name.

Bill Traylor's Dog

What she wanted now
was something primitive,
something like Bill Traylor's dog
the one he had drawn
two years ago on cardboard
from the refrigerator box
and painted
with black poster paint,
a dog with a tail
curved over his back
like a handle
on a whistling tea kettle
in which she could boil water
for a porcelain cup
of blackberry tea,
a dog with the eye
of a fish on a gilt plate,
an eye that could look up at her
but wouldn't see,
a dog with ears
like a mountain perked
to hear all the other dogs
scratching at its sides,
a dog with a stud
slung under his boat belly
like a rudder
that knew where to go
and when to turn,
a dog with a tongue
flat between his jaws
like a wafer,

a dog with little feet without nails,
as if Bill had tried to draw his shoes
but didn't know how,
feet like lumps,
outlined but unpainted
because he had run out of tempera,
little feet that weren't there at all
until she bought a crayon.

Henry Moore's *Three Motives Against a Wall*

The first is your mother seated on her bronze chest
and stripped to a ballet slipper. All that is left of her red hair
is an open mouth. The right arm which was so strong
and so beautiful has withered to a soldier's stump,
and the left fused into her thigh so that her whole body
becomes the opening through which you sink.

Beside her sits your father who could not dance,
and even now you cannot tell whether his stomach wells
desire or some other strange discomfort like a prayer.
Perhaps he is not your father, but your father's mother
with a bag of groceries slung in front of her
like a child. He is asking, she is asking why you sing.

And the third, the standing thing, maybe it becomes you
or maybe a bird who bears your father's wings.
You are holding his feathers like a shield,
you are the clumsy creature that waddles goose
or gander, your anatomy slipping into the other,
bone to blossom, rib to ring.

And behind you, what seems most important:
the wall with its irregular windows held like tuning forks
and the pitch you can not see through or even will to see
and the way light plays its sharp surfaces, its flat sting.

Green Snake Riding the Back of the Kitchen Chair
(after Frank Stella)

The garter snake wrapped its roadway
around the rungs of the kitchen chair,
and you said, racetracks, but whoa,

just because a man goes to university
doesn't mean he can tell
switchbacks from chicanery,

and the kitchen chair
had already acquired that cloudlike lightness
that characterized our flight

from Jarama to Zen.   I was beginning
to see there were circuits beneath sensuality,
though how to get there I could not guess,

for we had begun our spiraling descent
down into Spain where the black bulls
breathe gold rings in the Iberian fog

and I knew that before the race was over
I would begin to bleed, intimacy
sliding into someone else's dream.

Rabid Animals

When your job takes you
to Salem, Syracuse,
Sacramento and I am alone
with the child,

the head of the plaster woman
comes from wherever she came from
and floats across the quilt,
the disembodied Bianca.

You used to say your students
left her on the doorstep as a joke,
or sometimes a fruit bat or turkey
dropped her (I think it was the way

her earrings hung down, two bird cages
in Pompeii), and then there was her helmet
which neither you nor Shakespeare
could satisfactorily explain.

It's not warm-blooded mammals
or green oranges she brings,
but something that keeps hanging
to my nightgown like doubt:

perhaps I will not be able
to get to the doctor in time,
because you do not believe me,
perhaps I shall die sane.

Judy said this really big man,
two-hundred and seventy pounds of him,
came to the internist yesterday,
tried to pick up a dead raccoon

with a garbage bag, and the plastic slipped.
Do you know how many rabid shots
it takes to stop saliva on a sore?
He didn't even have to be bitten.

Every night there's a cat
who doesn't run when Johnny comes
to separate the paper from the glass,
and Karen says there's a dog in a ditch

foaming at the lips—
her youngsters poked its fur to pieces—
and now every night I look, bats bash
the headlights with their teeth.

The Sky Like Cobblestone

The cold sky
hangs on your face
like a stone beard

and, looking up,
you see the cobbled road
through which the stone queen fell,

the clouds torn
by her satin shoes,
the fog that did not hold her.

You have fallen too
through something thicker than mist,
something like spun glass,

and formed a fissure
in the gauze of the worm,
its star head tightening.

So what has the sky
to do with you, tied as you are
to your dog by a chain?

From your mouth
cold stones
cobble the air

and a mourning dove
drops her smooth gray pebbles
through your fingers.

She is hunching in the high elm
which you would call an oak
if you were honest

and the jay is crying
what it always cries,
thief, thief.

That Same Prayer

Yesterday morning,
rain and the thin priest
and the altar boy,
whose mother
drives him
from shrine
to shrine
so that he can sling
the morning wafer
like incense
on a chain,
splatters the news
to the sidewalk
like the smooth rush
of a baptismal bowl,
someone must drink
the altar wine
before it wastes,
we cannot
pour it
out.

And this
morning
that same boy
moves as slowly
as water rolling
down a wheat stem,
perhaps his mother is sick
or too late for the cafe
where she serves coffee

to men who work
in rain,
and so he holds himself carefully
like a pregnant woman
in a shower,
unwilling to risk
more water
than already rolls
his plump stomach,
his forehead
wet and shiny
like the man
in the classifieds
who wanted someone
over 50,
bald or beer-bellied,
it didn't matter,
I suppose you think
the rain is lonely,
but some don't care
if death when she comes
is a woman
empty of child
the rain
a fat gut
teeming with radishes.
The red-bellied robins
are jeering as if they
were pears,
so many cerements
straining on the line,
and a bird
I cannot identify

is warbling mercy
in the wet thistles,
perhaps a gold finch
like wild drops
of ale
singing in the seeds
that would unsex the world
and fall again
as the lightest mantle,
as rain.

Turning Fifty
    (for Richard)

The way we say it, turning fifty, as if
age is a direction, left or wrong, and we
can turn right around instead
of belly up, go back to where we startled,

leap again before we lean. Suppose
the doe who knew no turning
did not have to lie on the road's edge—
maybe we would not need

those elegant deceptions men wrap
in white sheepskin and tissue
like linen handkerchiefs. Turn the joker over.
Send him back to jail. I remember a game

in which we used miniature wrenches
to fix a leaky deck, I used to cheat,
though time's not love's fool either.
This month my hair is turning gray

as if it could turn sand or midas
and when I turn the faucet ,
the water spits—someone's tampering
with the pipes, and no one warned me

though off and on through all my life
I've filled the bathtub with safe water
and gone to bed a little sad.
Maybe we must turn old leaves,

turn a trick, pull the hoary rabbit from the hat,
or just turn tail and run the fishnet hose.
Yesterday I drank a wine the shade of shad:
I cannot say I liked it.

Women of Uncertain Age

Although we have not given up that odious grace, comparison,
by which we measured and were measured for so many years,
we know that silence becomes despair and lies . . . continuance,

and so we call to each other like well-feathered birds
you look so thin, that color becomes you
and some days in the bathroom mirror we see, by a trick

of memory or light or imagination, that face that brought
the houses down and believe once more for a moment
that just the right shade of pink will take us there.

But we know we have moved into another house
where the only audience to our chicanery is ourselves
and that no facelift or tummytuck can suck in the spirit,

and yet we examine the way another's body holds its shape
or the shape of someone we were a few days ago before our
    breasts,
our hips, our mouths began their giving and their giving way.

Vending Machine

It was one of those days when her body
felt more like a vending machine

than an engine of desire
and so she was thinking about George

smoothed flat and face-up
and wondering if Martha had said, please,

Mr. President, take out the wooden teeth,
but then she remembered George was impotent

(or was it sterile?), she had noticed
some machines reject bills with ragged corners

and he had said once too often
she wasn't getting older, just better,

maybe she shouldn't make
the mechanical whirl and growl,

just decide whether to keep the legal tender
or spit it out. The truth was,

spending himself the way he did
he hadn't noticed she was getting gray.

But that was no excuse:
she didn't like so much change inside herself.

The Dynamics of Cold

I woke alone
on a cold shore,
the moon shivering
in the sea,

and you took off
your shirt
and wound it
round my waist

so that time
began running
towards the black-
capped gulls.

Your heart
was so full
of bluefish
I put on

your gloves
to draw blood
back
into your fingers.

Then solitude
rushed in
the window
and we slept.

Who will
forget me
when you
are gone?

Tod und Leben

I do not know why this morning
I should imagine us like this:
I wrapped in the quilt of red patches,

my skin blue with loss, and you,
sadder than I have ever seen you,
your massive head resting between

my shoulder blades. We are holding
each other but I do not know who
is dying, we cannot see each other's face

and your arm has taken on the burnish
of muscled water. You've wrapped
an embroidered kimono around your thighs,

I cannot bear to see what you are saying.
The body apparelled becomes the bird,
and where do the fingers of the unborn

find their bread, perhaps you are leaving
and I have nothing to wrap my belly
but this sheet.

Departure

How difficult
the morning
before you leave
for any place
to say anything
important,
wanting,
as you do,
to surprise yourself
with the old fan
on the kitchen table.

So you pack away
your notes
in the silverware drawer
and forget the advice:
stay home,
dig your own potatoes.
You have named
every fleabane
in the garden.

Yet before you go,
you want to apologize,
explain how low
the domestic sky
has fallen
and how the trees
are ascending
into smog.

And then, of course,
you want to climb them
one last time,
monkey up the dead willow
and look out,
over the temperate canopy,
catch the roof of your
neighbor's house,
where, yes,
her red-headed son
is lying in the light,
his shoulders
shimmering
against the mahogany leaves.

Maybe he is sitting
there now,
rubbing the green dawn
into his thighs,
maybe he is looking up
and waving
as if you were
seventeen—
for the moment
you are the only two
in this familiar world
amazed
at your leaving.

But had you never left
that first time,
twenty-two years ago,
you would not

know now
that it is his freckled skin
that is beautiful,
you would have
wanted him to
say something
significant to you,
as you want,
even now,
to shout something
through the limbs,
something that he will remember
every place he descends.

When you come back,
nothing will be the same,
your sheets
will smell different,
the sun will wear
a strange cerise
and when you
climb the elm
the boy
you wanted to touch
will have disappeared.

Loitering in Air

The leaves, two or three
still clinging to the top of the oak
like wooden angels jacking up a stick
make me think

it is not flying we talk about,
but the long fall in which we float,
as once, looking at my watch,
I saw time stop for no reason.

What tricks I've tried since then
to stretch a moment, hold
the mechanical hand from moving,
silk a second into a second coming—

and yet there is only this gliding,
the flat wings on a jerked string,
the awkward stable below
and a black goat fleeing.

Oh stars falling from us
like the brain of heaven receding,
think what shepherds breathe
in this desert of methane and dust.

What shall we wear
to protect us—some sequined
and slit incarnation
that leaves us hanging,

for the moment, upside down
on a frayed rope, our bodies still perfect
and muscular as any circus acrobat,
our legs opening to the light?

A Note About the Author

Lois Marie Harrod is the author of two previous volumes of poetry, *Every Twinge a Verdict* (Belle Mead Press, 1987) and *Crazy Alice* (Belle Mead Press, 1991), and a chapbook *Green Snake Riding* (New Spirit Press, 1994). Her poems have appeared in many journals among them *Carolina Quarterly, Southern Poetry Review, The Literary Review, Zone 3, Green Mountains Review, Prairie Schooner* and *American Poetry Review.* She is a recipient of a 1992-93 fellowship from the New Jersey Council of the Arts. A high school English teacher, she also supervises Creative Writing at the New Jersey Governor's School of the Arts. She and her husband Lee Harrod live in Hopewell, New Jersey.

Cover Art: *Horseshoe Crab*, Wendell Jeffrey
Author Photo: Ann Holt

This book was designed by Live Oak. It is set in Garamond type and manufactured by Bookcrafters.